Miraculous Hours

MIRACULOUS HOURS

MATT RADER

NIGHTWOOD EDITIONS
ROBERTS CREEK, BC
2005

Nightwood Editions
R.R. #22, 3692 Beach Ave.
Roberts Creek, BC
Canada V0N 2W2

Edited for the house by Silas White
Typesetting by Carleton Wilson
Title page design by Ben Didier (www.iheartnoise.com/pork)

We gratefully acknowledge the support of the Canada Council for the Arts and the British Columbia Arts Council for our publishing program.

Printed and bound in Canada.

LIBRARY AND ARCHIVES CANADA CATALOGUING IN PUBLICATION

Rader, Matt, 1978–
        Miraculous hours / Matt Rader.

Poems.
ISBN 0-88971-201-8

        I. Title.

PS8585.A2825M57 2005   c811'.6   C2005-901393-1

Dear Melanie,

CONTENTS

BREATH

THE LAND BEYOND

and the miraculous hours of childhood wander in darkness

– Mark Strand

PROLOGUE

First, I rap the wall
above my desk
and divine the stud.

Then, I choose a hammer
and drive a six-inch spike
through the gyprock.

The dog digs under the fence.

A bird flies into the window.

A small red blister
at the site of the wound.
A whisker of blood.

My eyelids twitch.

The walls are ready to talk.

EXODUS

Exodus

St. Patrick's Day in the New World, the wind
hunting the hills. My parents climb into my father's year-

old Ford pickup and drive the lake road
down the Malahat to Wayne Brown's place

in Shawnigan Village. My mother is swollen
and nervous and spends the evening holding her belly

in the corner of the kitchen, sprawled
on an old leather chair the Van Barneveld boys stole

from the Mill Bay Inn—just picked it up
and walked out—while Wayne and my dad drink

a couple Luckys and smoke a joint
on the pack porch. It's warm for mid-March. "Strange

Fruit" on the stereo, housefly on the kitchen table.
My mother wants to fall asleep, she will later tell me,

just curl up and go inside herself, kick my ass
into the world. She is sure I am a boy,

the way I will not leave her body. Today,
she tells Wayne's wife Deirdre,

is my Grandfather Langley's birthday. Today
is the day they drove the snakes out of Ireland, says Deirdre,

and they both laugh, knowing full well it isn't
true. The men don't come inside all night.

They piss in the yard and when Mum asks for a ride
home they let Deirdre help her out to the truck.

Dad drives and Wayne sits in the middle. Mum
rolls down the window. They listen to Woody Guthrie

sing "1913 Massacre" and part of "The Biggest Thing
Man Has Ever Done" before the tire goes, the truck ruts

in the midnight gravel. There are no streetlamps
on the lake road, no moon above the trees.

Dad curses the corroded flashlight batteries. The scent
of manure and freshwater. My mother gets out

of the truck, places her hands on the hood,
fingers the dirty heat from the engine. Tonight,

I am due to be born. On the horizon, two columns
of light approach. Mum holds out her thumb.

Hang on Baby, she whispers, *we're almost home—*

EARLY EPISODES

after C.D. Wright's "Bent Tones"

There was a dance at the Big House.
In the motel a girl was learning her trade.

A woman drove herself to the hospital,
rubbing her thighs to bring back the blood.

The snow kept everything in place, freeze-framed.
Before his truck drove into a lamp-pole

she chained the dog to the rotting maple.
Stinging nettle on the stove-top. In the air, coiled rope.

When the Angels ran the airfield everything trembled—
the woodsmoke they blew through, the hermit thrush,

reception on the RCA. With her mother's ears
she could hear Little Ben
missing the toilet bowl for the umpteenth time.

Dogs

The dogs slid through the door and up the stairs
like ghosts, unnoticeable save the sharp pitch of heat

in the house. Palmer lay passed out on the couch,
did not see the black muzzled mutt approach,

lift its tender snout to his mouth. In the kitchen I turned from
        the stove
to catch a sloe-eyed hound click onto the linoleum—

I hit the first with the tea kettle and the second
with a fry pan from the dish rack, two-handed like a baseball bat,

kept swinging it madly so the third held back at the edge of
        the carpet,
hackled and ready to attack if I took a step closer.

Outside, the sun slipped behind the evergreens and Tom Parker's
truck backfired in the alley. I felt the baby kick,

bared my teeth the way dogs did—

FRIENDSHIP

Little survives a broken neck. The way the deck steps
quaked under the weight of our chase, of our descent:
my narrow escape from James' grubby hands must have
spooked the knot of slow-breathing, preening kittens
that lounged on the blood-warmed concrete below us.
And I guess it was the fall of my shadow between the stairs
that froze the only white one where it did—mid-panic
in front of the last step—caught in the drop of my body
promised by that sudden black. I could not stop myself.
What was about to happen it seemed had already happened.
James was gaining fast, fat fingers only a fist from my back.
It would be a lie to say I heard him laugh, but I know he did,
the way one does when shocked out of thought, when overcome
by momentum and understanding: he knew even before
I did—barely felt it, her head snap back, the mush of her
throat crushed beneath my heel, the bloom of blood in her
mouth, both dumb and painfully articulate. James held her
while she choked. I thought I should cry or try to explain,
but I just stood there and neither of us spoke.

CRUELTY

The girl we call Missy lives in the pea-green two-storey
on the corner. Her real name is Jane or Mary, and she's known
for eating cat food from a bag her mother keeps in the closet

of their unfinished basement, which is all gyprock and plumbing,
and a sea of unwashed clothes next to the litter box
where we wrestle. She and I fight at school, but on the block

we're friends, except when she stinks or her face is filthy
with bruises, which is often, and then we throw stones
or ignore her until she goes home. Never seen her father,

but her mum is fat and pale and has hair on her chin.
Missy and I take our clothes off in the bush at the end of the road,
look each other over. Not much to distinguish one from the other

at this age. Eventually all is forgotten except our skin
and the teaming hump of ants we are teaching now
about destruction. Missy would like to touch me

but I will not let her. An ant clings between my thumb
and forefinger. Missy pulls it apart, leg by leg, until it is
only head and *thorax*, she says. Missy is moving at the end of

the summer to a base called Cold Lake where it snows
most seasons. Today, we nurse honeysuckle and do not speak of her
leaving, though it is something we both understand better

than the feeling which rises in us when Missy closes
my hand, crushes the ant.

PICKUP

An industrial pack-horse, worn down and shot,
left to rot in the pea-gravel at the edge of the yard. For years

it crouched there in front of the shop, un-thought-of
except as a distant project or parts in a pinch for

dollars. A pain in the ass to scramble under in search of
a lost ball or stray puck, we avoided it

the way one might a patch of stinging nettle or devil's club,
instinctually and without comment. And then on a lark

the year we learned to smoke, Dana tried the driver's-side handle
and opened the door to a dank and mildewed inner dark

we clambered into and hotboxed, watched what out-there
        there was
disappear in the fogged-up windows

of our thoughts. We might have been explorers,
our cigarettes like tiny torches: when we had a haul

the whole cab glowed: the spill of spiders stalled
above the dashboard, the hawk moth that shuddered,

our smoke like roads unfolding before us—

SKULL

Down in the swamp an uprooted tree,
its skirt of earth a shadow lobe of brain,
fetid and root-veined, a boot print in the mud.
Mosquitoes, like words taken to heart, sworn,
addicted, hot for your blood. Pant.
Water on your tongue, spit bugs.

And this table here in the clearing.
And these chairs sinking into the earth.
Some kind of outpost, retreat, abandonment.
All the garbage: gas can, condom rubber,
pencil. And where the brain was, draw
a puddle of mud and tarps, a blanket.

DIVINER

Ants in the dishwasher and the flicker on the east wall divining
        food:
slowly, the house disassembled, consumed, transformed into
        energy

and dream in the cells of insect and bird. Asleep in the yard,
an open book on my chest, print at rest on my skin: tattoo,
        fossil, birth-

mark. I dream the dream the hawk spies at the edge of the airfield,
trembling like the first bubbles of life in the sun, primordial
        pools of

air flooding the dry grass, the spot where the circle ends or
        appears
to: A box in Dad's shop marked Miscellaneous Persona: birth
        certificate,

SIN card, Wellbutrin; then naked in the bathroom, reading my
        body
in the mirror: *I remind you of the man who invented himself.* Hidden

in a spruce tree, a crow child speaks and speaks her thirst for
        flight,
talks the marrow from my bones, the soft dark truth of human
        form.

FROG LUST

In fields and ditches
deep through the marshlands,
mad and abandoned, otherworldly,
that long thought of pulse-kiss blown across space
by a faraway species, and we three brothers
night-blind, enticed like satellites
through hemlock and bird
sanctuary to find it. Listen:
on the banks of the swamp,
the shadowy salal and deerfoot
jungle around us, and us
gone trancelike, mesmerized
by the come-hither ballad
of a creature in decline. Owl cries
arc across the soundscape, rocket
out of fuel; the odd dog howls
or moans behind a fence-line;
car tires purr the beach-road.
Never so together
or alone, my brothers and I
shoulder to shoulder, our torsos
only deeper amoebas of dark,
that old spring mojo
hard on through the trees into the atmosphere
and breathing in our ears:

Organism. Organism. Organism. . .

PIKE

Muckrake, mucker, silt on a set of sticks
picked from the lake depths you fly through—

Water-wolf, jackfish, mud-child
like us, detritus from the early minutes of manufacturing

and raw materials. Jut-jawed, thorn-toothed,
hook-crazed as a lost boot. What purchase holds you

now, noosed in a knot of water, draws me deeper
to sleep and follow—

Baseball

Stepped to the plate and tapped the Louisville against your heel,
knocked a little dust from your cleats, loosened your wrists,
then caught a glimpse of the catcher's eye, cross-hatched
behind his mask, a familiar glint or eye-smirk you almost
     remembered,
that you could have sworn you'd seen before but were unsure—
You crouched over home and waved the wood a couple times
like a wand. Then the pitcher batted his eyelashes and shook
     his cap
and the whole scene started to shake from your brain, to melt
away like old snow on a car window, revealing a memory
half-then and half-now: that same catcher as a kid,
standing on your balcony with your pet rabbit in his mitts,
     dangling it
over the edge, that same glint daring you to stop him with a fist
or speak out, your mother in the kitchen preparing sandwiches,
your brothers down the hall cutting bags of dope, you weren't
     alone
but you froze: a knuckleball, no spin, a pitch with rabbit ears
pinned up in the wind, with jack-feet pedalling hard against the
     end—
and when you remembered the slugger in your hands
brought it off your shoulder and turning on your back foot
connected now with then, described an arc known as revenge—

FIRESETTER

Pyro plain and simple: I build fires. Behind the Safeway
a man touched me in a way I will not speak of. I burned him
alive with lighter fluid and a match I struck across my shoe.
It is a curse and a gift, handed down, bequeathed, inherited,
like clairvoyance, alcoholism, the impulse to violence. A medium
between the elements. I once met a man who felt water
through a stick, wanted to feel me too. I set him ablaze
with a bottle of rum and the cigarette that smoked in his mouth.
Watch as the spider curls like paper, the snake shrivels
through the alphabet. There is language in the click of a lighter,
epiphany in a blister of skin. I was not always like this
you must remember: dangerous, kindled, combustible. It was
the man in the cloakroom, the oil on the ocean, the magnifying
glass and bone-dry grasses, electricity, paint thinner, bottled
oxygen. Life is a kind of burning, a moving towards ashes,
so lift your hands and be gone. Behind the school the oak trees
eat themselves from root to leaf until they vanish like ghosts
in the heat and thickening smoke. Do not overestimate
my control: fire is a fist in my throat I cannot swallow or spit
out. It has a mind of its own and every breath I take is fuel
to help it grow, rampage, consume, consume, explode.

Miraculous Hours

The stutter-speech of sprinklers in the neighbour's yard.
The whisper language of lawns and moths. Tonight,

on the front porch striking matchsticks with our thumbs,
the quick report of light doused out on our tongues,

it's the trick that speaks volumes: forget phosphorus, friction,
the miracle of combustion, it is how you hold fire

in your mouth then snuff it out like idle conversation.

The Water Tower

Set back on the ridge through a maze of cedar-
slash and gravel-track: as kids we'd ride our bikes out there

past the last house on the street and catch air off rocks
or primitive ramps kicked together with dirt and sticks, anything

we could pop a wheelie onto and pedal over,
the big blue silo looming above us, barely noticed

except as a place to meet and practice our graffiti,
the names of our classmates scrawled across the smooth steel
        base,

along with any rumours, secrets, malicious gossip that we knew
or could think up, the latest curse word heard or sexual organ

learned of—it could have held gasoline or munitions
or cattle feed for all I knew but I liked the sound it emitted

when I put my ear to it and my brothers bombarded the far side
with rocks, something like a wounded ox

crossed with a rocket set off underwater, how it reverberated
in my jaw and down my neck for several seconds after

the echoes stopped. And then as teenagers it was the spot
on Friday nights to drink and get high, settle any outstanding
      fights

like men, in the dark, out of sight of cops, parents, nosy
      neighbours
who might pull us apart at the first sign of blood. Condom
      wrappers,

cigarette butts, a pair of jockey underwear hanging from an
      elder bush,
the carcass of a cat flayed and laid out over a milk crate—

At first the tower was only what surrounded it,
but after Katie was raped in the back of Kyle's truck

while we watched through the canopy window, the thing itself
was all we could think of: a giant blue bullet, a torpedo

unexploded in the earth, waiting for one wrong move
to blow us into what we were and were not—

FALLING

Clipped my skull on the lip of the bridge
as I plunged feet-first into the anxious river.
My teeth jawed together, all castanet
or clamshell, crunched my tongue to pulp.
I couldn't talk, or scream, or lift a finger.
Couldn't remember why I was there or where
amongst all the falling my body had gone.
Rivulets of red ribboned my head like an insect-
painter's quick study of the wingless human—
The Faller—a gesture-drawing in blood and air.
Here's how I picture it: limbs all stutter and wheel
in the rioting wind, all seizure of sign language
and panic-dance, eyes scrolled back, calculating
velocity by distance, the time left to swallow
or spit before impact. Never mind the fear
or embarrassment, I pissed my pants just for
the warmth in my crotch, that one last sloppy kiss.
Falling and falling is lonely business.

ROBIN

Tuneless suitor, unpartnered,
pitchless in this late spring evening
with its jackal-heat and wind-noose,
your song hanged in your gullet,
dangling out of time, dripping
with un-hoped-for hope
that your lover will return
from the cat's gut and bogey mouth.
Even the worms are at home
in the darkening earth
coupling, dividing themselves
for company and numbers,
preparing for the flood.
It would be easy to give up
but for the despairing and obsessed
instrument of your heart,
with its valves and chambers
and Machiavellian pipes,
its terrible there-for-life drone notes,
its devoted unholy commotion.

BROOKLYN CREEK

An oil painter coloured the creek red and slew
The steelhead. Ever since, we've been coming back

From this. We never learned to avoid the thin ice
That curdled each winter in the swampy parts,

Kept filling our boots with water and creek mud
While tadpoles grew legs, stepped outta sedge

Full of song and brave lungs. There was no question
Who threw the first punch, who cut the willow switch,

We were only children. In the winter run-off,
Kent rode an inner tube through the culvert.

Kent rode an inner tube through the culvert
And down the fish ladder. He was never seen again.

Pond skaters pocked the creek skin, and our screams
Drowned the water babble, never to be heard again.

The sun rested in cedar boughs. Mud wasps
Binged on juice boxes. The fish never spawned again.

It was always the beginning of the end. The cursive
Snake wrote his name on the water, never to be read again.

In our fingers whistled tall grass. Thistles bloomed,
Paul pricked his brain. The moon sank never to float again.

Paul pricked his brain. The moon sank never to float again.
Algae painted the rushes and insects jotted their thoughts

In the journeying water. We played make-believe
On the creek banks until our mothers called us home

Under planets and street lamps. In the quivering twilight
First crushes were born and died. We children of

Brooklyn, in our sopping clothes, never wanted
To be dry. Another soaker. We were wet with questions

Of who and what long before the poses how and why
Were ever struck. Lightning by any other . . . Luck.

poised in the heron neck hushed tripwired and set triggered to
        stab at and devour bullhead after bullhead
blink-quick or quicker still whip-lightning swift morsels tracked
        by shadow by motion plucked from the ocean
to whet the gullet get at the empty fill in the stomach

hooped and hewing the air a hawk caught in a gyre whirlpooled
        and lathed near tabooed turned to a talon-point a kill and
        still turning
a vole-beat in its ear a hare-breath any timid rodent-movement
        or clearing-step to narrow on and nail to dive at to focus
        to bleed in a field
a jugular-death prey-perfect painless save a bubble of blood in
        its mouth the choke in its breath

root-beck well-vein water-skeeter come blood cell in the creek
        leaf palsy where no hand can be seen messing in the tree
        only wind-strings pulling
a whistle through limb and trunk sinewed and long insinuated
        by echo and canyon muffled by undergrowth sewn in
        the wood

TREVER'S SONG

in memory of Trever Harris

In the space between slip and fall, the asphalt sky prickled
        with stars,
he felt a noise break in his heart, blood-rushed and ecstatic,
        jazz-boned,
the low swell of a saxophone gone berserk, a frenetic constellation
of notes jerked from his dreams and set earborne above the earth.

He heard dirt-tones and blood-chords, hunger-phrases and bone
        notes all
shaken like a gin martini and woven into flannel shirts, a muddy
        bike ride
through his life hung as a mobile in the last of the summer nights,
the spooled sound of his body unspun, let loose, rain over Hornby
        Island.

And in that instant a light fired in his eye, and he spied his
        reflection
glimmer in the crystal flesh of the night, shatter-wise and
        dumbstruck,
silent in the bosom of the rushing wind, and soul tied like a
        marionette
to the sky, a huge net of sound parachuting him unharmed to
        the ground.

NIGHT-SWIMMER

The sunburnt moon a cradle in the treetops,
and bats like sudden rifts in the fabric of night.
We stand naked at the edge of the pool, our bodies
carried away by horsefly and no-see-um.
Our days have marked us in different ways:
the fine hairs on your belly move in the moonlight
like whispers in a crowd, entice the bramble scar
from my chest: the softening of old wounds.
Like spiders, we rest our toes on the water,
test the surface for tension.
                              Without a word,
you slip into the river, sliver through the dark echo of
outer space, a million years closer to the steelhead
who drew this midnight bath. In your wake,
fir needles map your path, the lantern-light of
your skin soaks the pool. Your body rings,
sluices the river choir *sotto voce*, folds me
like a prayer for harmony into the water.

FAITH

Stored Dad's ashes in a mason jar—
swept them from the funeral pyre
after it cooled, bits of bone and tooth,
the smell of salmon somehow.
Kept him in the living-room
fireplace and had no more fires.
Tried not to look during breakfast.
Looked. Duct-taped the glass,
then peeled it off before Mum saw.
I wanted to make him an hourglass,
my sisters thought a pillow or shaker,
someone said beach. At night
I stole pinches of foot, dashes
of hand, refilled it with sand,
and buried him toe-by-finger
in potted earth and rose seed.
In this way he came back to me:
root and thorn, rosehip, became
jam that smelled of fishmeal,
forty-one white petals I pressed
between the pages of my hand.

Clearing Out

Perched like a gargoyle at the gable end of the house,
feet firmly fixed on the rough tar and shingles, ankles
angled to the pitch and run of the roof, I was stooped

and anchored by the job I had to do: guard the gutter-
spout from a winter's worth of soggy leaves and grime,
while a steady push of lake water pulsed from the hose-

mouth the entire length of the house. It was annual
end-of-winter work and I was obligated to it since
I professed no sense of vertigo the way my brothers did,

no strange impulse to a header just for the hell of it.
Hands numbed to dumb animals that fumbled
and scooped the grungy residue and hurled it earth-

wards like black-wet epithets on chores and work.
Couple minutes and the cramps kicked in, so it was
all shift and squat and shift again, each new position

a gamble against gravity and wind. Who would do this
for less than a case of Keith's and a pack of JPS—minus
two sticks—slipped into his coat pocket? Truth is,

I craved the distance, the quick two-storey trip
to a whole new perspective—doe-eyed satellite dishes,
antennae like birthday wishes—good ear tuned

to the trickle turned thrum of water, clear and true.

BREATH

From alveoli, bronchi, trachea—
speech cousin, gravity descendent,
as all things are eventually.

Tide plan. Moon thought.

The breather born in a split second
switch from water breath and uterine lung,
to lift, draw, expand, rush—

oxygen bloom in blood.

Breathing, we share ourselves.
Forced-air pant, helixed with dog hair and rat skin,
adenine, cytosine, thymine, from a vent
above our bed, we breathe the house-
genome, the long line
come cycle of life in the air,
translated to blood by lung,
then rivered through vein and capillary
to be used, and become us,

                              addendum. In the morning
the room's rank. Breathing,
send me back.

Refrigerator buzz. Mice-step
in walls. Sleep-talk.
Sound-as-breath, inference
only a breather could understand.
The crust swell of apple pie
pulled hot from the oven.
Blitzkreig of a popped balloon across the kitchen.
Sunset. Moonrise. Eclipse.

The gown of air sewn by fingers
as a rock lifts from the garden,
the drag
              and fall
                          and ribbon,
all arc and arm, trailing from hip to head,
shunting dry saliva-breath in a huff,
from lung to mouth to wrist to palm to tip of

finger,
        release—

THE LAND BEYOND

ELECTRIC CHAIR BY ANDY WARHOL

Ladies and gentlemen, prepare to be shocked
and amazed. This sturdy piece of oaken furniture,
fashioned with the love and grace of a master
carpenter—a real character—is expertly wired
with the very latest in solid state circuitry.
Complete with electrodes for the head and feet,
adjustable backrest, drip pan, Plexiglas seat,
and primed and painted with a high-gloss epoxy
developed for space, it is a state-of-the-art system
for all your electrocution needs. Plug-in
components, and a dose of pentobarbital sodium
no more than one half hour prior to execution,
makes no-hassle handling for any Jack Ketch
stuck awaiting the word to work the switch—

HIGHLAND FIELDS

Belly down in the grassy mud at the edge of the pitch,
the boy cocked the rifle the moment we emerged from the trail
and trained it on my brother, the long gaze of the barrel

like a nail that fixed us in space. Across the field the blacktails
tilted their heads at the click of metal and a crow staggered
between the uprights. I figured we'd spooked the kid

mid-act maybe waiting to tag a gull rooting in the ditch
or thumbing a porno he'd nicked from a corner-store shelf
so I lifted my hand to wave hello and felt his finger tighten

at the motion, one eye pinched shut, the other bearing down
like a locomotive along the rail of the gun. That afternoon
the moon watermarked the horizon

and a shatter of juncos broke like ice from the willow scrub—

WOODS

Night oozed through the streets and the chain-link skirt
of the public-works yard, flattered itself

in the owl's pupil, spilled a thousand thousand silent shrews
onto the forest floor, wretched a muscle of worms

Night was in the throat of the crow who swallowed greedily
and disappeared deeper into himself

Night moved but night was not the wind
that cut like light, that dusted the air with needle and whisper

that looted and uprooted trees, ransacked branches
rustled the deer heart, scattered the titmouse

Night was not your voice that pleaded for direction
nor your breath that thistled my neck

when we stopped to listen for and spot the flicker
hammering in a treetop like the dull drum of our thoughts—

the earth lapped our feet and age collected in the storied moss.

WOLF LAKE

It was down that road he brought her, still
in the trunk of his car. That September
the horseflies were murder and I remember
the dust of the logging trucks rolling off
the mountain seemed to travel forever
over the valley like insects or weather.
Everything seemed darker that month,
that year. How many times have we been down
this road to snag some trout, to poach
some timber: the old Ford pickup rutting
in the gravel where the road washed out
the previous winter and Pete rolling a joint
in the passenger seat, always so anxious
to meet a bear or cougar, something at least
potentially vicious, out there in the woods,
where his screams and shouts would do him
no good except to spook the creature
or get it riled up and maybe that way
he'd get to use the Winchester I kept
resting in the gun rack behind our heads.
But in the end, we never saw much—
a few deer, a muskrat, the odd raven
we always heard first, its steel-on-steel
wing-carving of the late summer air. We did
a lot of talking and swallowing of beer,
but sometimes we liked to pretend
we weren't really there, imagine if
we were quiet enough and didn't move

much, the world would forget about us
and get on with its business: the fir trees would
uproot and plot revenge on the chainsaw,
the fossilized logs spiking the lake would
rise up on the back of the last dinosaur.
It's what we wished for but it never happened
and after a while we'd split the final round
or pack up the tackle and toss it in the back
of the truck, maybe smoke a last j—. I remember
we always smelled of fish or sawdust
by the end of the day, and there was a tape
of Stan Rogers we liked to play on the drive out—
which was what we were doing in the twilight
of that afternoon, when we turned the corner
and spotted the rust-bitten Chrysler stopped
 on the shoulder with him hunched over,
hauling a figure up and out of the trunk.
He paused at the sound of the truck, but didn't
look up and we could tell by the hair
and slender arms and fingers it was
a woman he had draped over him like a rug.
As we got closer he started for the woods
and I thought I spotted blood on the hood
of the car. I braked hard and as we slowed up,
the wheels locked and the back end fishtailed
in the dust. My head rushed, thinking
what end are we about to come to here,
as he dumped her body and started to run.
I admit to a little fear, but Pete just laughed
and reached back for the gun—

NOSTALGIA

Harris is speeding, but he does it so naturally
we don't even notice. Rain, the first in forty days,
shoots through the open windows of the rusty Le Barron
like confused insects. Young girls in bikinis
slip out front doors and lay spread-eagle
on warm concrete driveways. Lawns look scorned
by the turn in weather and the air smells sweetly
of dust, and tar, and acid rain. I am riding shotgun,
and when I crack a Lucky, the three guys
in the backseat do the same. *Appetite for*
Destruction winds itself through the tape player
like an old story you never get tired of hearing. It's
late in the afternoon, late August. No one has any idea
where we are going. Harris is speeding,
but like I say, he does it so naturally we don't
even notice. We hit the hill leaving town and Jackie
sparks up in the back seat, wipers streaking wasp guts
across the windshield. The road bends west
onto the dyke and beyond the black cloud
that hangs above the valley, the sun lies skewered
on the Island mountains. High tide at the throat of
the road, two Indian kids jigging for bullheads
off the shoulder. The scene in the film where
we cross the centre line and crash headfirst into
the family of four heading home for supper. Monsters,
they'll say. Axl gunning for the money note
in Paradise City. I feel better than I have in days

Scavenger Hunt

Some items are personal: the snapshot of us at the beach, drunk
        and naked
in the phosphorescence, that first kiss, shivering under the street
        lamp.

Others are practical: binoculars, stethoscope, every minute
we spent breathing on the telephone (I could do wonders with
        those).

And then there's the esoteric, the out-there, the just-plain-weird:
a strand of Woolman's neck hair, a bite of bologna in the shape of
        a deer.

Or the kicker, the topper, the one to watch for: a human heart,
        beating
or already stopped, doesn't matter. Nab that and it's over, you win.
        Hurry,

as soon as you get here the party begins—

The Land Beyond

our house is all tall grass and alder sapling,
broom scrub and blackberry bramble,
small neighbourhood of cedar,
odd hemlock and coniferous carcass,
deer-trail, foot-path, access-road.
We have lived here now one whole fall,
bordered by par-three Longlands and Crown Isle,
complete with gold-plated fire hydrants
and spiked (by neighbour) with dog
shit in the ninth—I don't
envy the jerk who makes that putt. I have
smoked dope between the ribs
of every house on our street,
while the ribs still showed. Before
the gyprock and vinyl and deadbolts,
I stole nails and two-by-fours from each lot,
stashed them in the couch grass and brome
where the deer sleep, dragged them
through mud on weekends
to an outpost at the edge of the bush:

three cedars locked together by metal and wood,
tucked out of sight by a fir-blind.
Here we smoke and have conversation,
shoot a constellation of aluminum cans
with pellet guns, chase rabbits.
This is plateau country. At night
frogs talk in the holding pond,
headlights blink down in the valley:
dead still, we imagine ourselves
lost not far from the edge of the trail,
and a small panic happens in my breast—
O Lord, don't let them find us.

Paradise Meadows

The blade blinked in the lover's moss at the edge of the trail,
and I stopped, reached down and touched it, half-buried in the
      boggy earth,

where the boy stumbled and lost his balance in the whitening
      snow,
the gash in his calf where the trap closed tied off
with a strip of canvas from his pants he could not make tight
      enough,

blood like huckleberries speckling the snow
and the sharp stink of the she-wolf he'd been tracking all
      afternoon in his nostrils,
her shadow shifting through the timbers,

the knife he used to free himself from the steel-grip still in his
      fist—

I wiped it on my sleeve and the sun jumped from tree to tree
like a small white flame, caught my face ablaze in the frame of
      the blade,
folded it and put it away—

CROW

              perched on the power line
and folded his wings. The drooling sky
clamped shut—a break in the weather
long enough for us to go out for a smoke,
take a stroll through the neighbourhood
parks and graveyard. War was on your mind
and for me it was that last stupid move
to lose my queen. In retrospect we were
underdressed for the time of year: my ears
burned red and didn't so much hurt
as went numb; you complained the lighter
didn't work, your fingers
able to fumble sparks
but no flame. People were out
walking their dogs and feeding the ducks—
one fellow was jogging around the block
backwards—neither of us could help but feel
a little awkward or lame the way we were
always unprepared where others seemed
to fare without complaint, us always unable
to predict or plan, or wager a decent guess.

Crow cawed and light shattered
on the still-wet asphalt. We peered at ourselves,
faceless in that almost-mirror of the street,
the skeleton trees blacking up behind us,
power lines quivering above—when we looked up,
Crow was gone. Storm-black clouds rolling off
the North Shore mountains towards us—

DUCKLINGS

A posse of dull upside-down light bulbs,
fuzzy and yolk-coloured,
they duck-stepped towards our bench
then stopped, periscoped their necks
and gave us the wide-eyed once-over,
before waddling in formation
a little closer. The bugs were bad,
lifting out of the lily pads
and creeping smartweed,
like airborne spores of offal
looking for new flesh to feast on
and seed—one was in my ear.
It was just the first move of the chess game
but neither of us wanted to play,
feeling these strange little half-bird things
watching us as they pecked
at the sunflower shells and cigarette butts
about our feet. It seemed they had no fear,
no country instincts to keep them away,
just citified feed-me brains
that mistook the stale stench of beer
and marijuana for something to eat.
They were cute in an ugly kind of way,
their molted mother at the edge of the lake,

dutifully looking on
with a broods-will-be-broods
expression on her face—I could see
we understood each other,
our shared love of the little ones—
until a mosquito landed on my collarbone,
began mining my marrow (or so it felt)
and I raised my hand to swat it dead,
palm open, fingers splayed—
that old lady duck didn't even hesitate,
just started towards us with a loud quack
that coincided with the smack of hand and chest,
and sent the ducklings into a mess
of directions and webbed feet
beating their best retreat to the lake,
while the mosquito buzzed by me
into the reeds, satisfied and safe.

PREPARATIONS

Broke the bird bath with a sledgehammer before the sun
got up and spent the rest of the morning draining
the goldfish barrel and burning it in the firepit. Have to
wonder what viruses or spores, what bugs
were borne off with the smoke or survived buried
in the ash and coal, gone dormant, but alive,
violent and unpredictable as volcanoes. Still,
we do what we can. Used to be
the crows were so noisy I couldn't sleep past seven.
Now silence is the thing that wakes me—the birds having been
poisoned or exposed, infected with a new blackness
that caused them to lose contrast I guess and disappear.
So it's an end to standing water in the backyard.
An end to composting the robins that storm
against the kitchen window as played by the wind
for a joke, an offering or omen laid crooked
and limp at the foot of the house. No more
evenings on the front porch reading or watching
the children skateboard or ride bikes in the street;

nights we go indoors to avoid the bugs and spray trucks
that roam the neighbourhood like ghosts
from the days of chemical warfare and plague.
Later today, I'll go down to the lake to count ducks—
some now turning up dead in the reeds—
the numbers used to track the disease as it deepens
and spreads species to species. Other volunteers
bag the bodies and take photographs
as if at a crime scene. For me it's an excuse
to get away from the house, to put my mind to use—
condition my memory for field and forest of the future,
for clearing or lakeshore, where all the fliers are
gone and only imperfectly remembered.

STREET CROSSING

after Tomas Tranströmer

Cars screech to a stop like a swarm of insects
humming on hold, transfixed by the eye
that hangs above the road, unblinking, electric, controlled.

And a breath below the asphalt, the dark loam
continues: frost-heaves in the roadwork, potholes,
the unborn forest taking hold—

Soyez Prudent

> *Hazardous Waves Can*
> *Sweep you off rocky headlands*
> *Suddenly flood beaches*
> > *crushing you in moving logs*
> > *catching you in currents*

> – sign at Wickaninnish Beach, Pacific Rim National Park

Behind us the sun maunders on the edge of the world,
the crooked white fingers of ocean which beckon us to our water
      home.
Slumped against the car door, sleep whispers in my ear like
      eyelashes
on a cheekbone; the constant lecture of surf through a crack
in the car window. We have been travelling for years now
it seems, caught in the slipstream of moving towards rest:
me taking care to look where I step, you taking care to see.

This morning packing the car, these are the things I thought
we'd need: towel, chair, plant guide—then drive all morning
to Long Beach and dream on the sand: the giant bonsai spruce
stroking their coifs in the wind, the gentle Japanese of sand fleas.
But waves can flood any beach, catch you in any current.
Now, my gut rises with the speedometer after each small climb,
pauses in my throat, falls away with the asphalt.

SLEEPWALKER

*

Spring and the pollen heavy on your eyelashes.
Every time you blink, bees like synapses. You hear
a high-pitched whine all day and you feel your hair
grow older. Night after night, in the bathroom
mapping the scars on your legs and weaving wigs.

*

Listen: whispers. Wolf piss in the garden,
soap carvings to keep the deer out, the breeze,
anything close. Your fingernails reach out.
Your own footsteps, and now someone
is after you. Every morning, run to work.

*

Baby teeth in a plastic cup. Chew the rim
for good luck and bury it beneath the birch tree.
You are being spoken to you feel you are
being spoken of. Hush. The philtrum,
the spot the Finger touched. Hush.

*

Tongue talks back to your thoughts and you
listen: bees in the middle of the street, too loaded
to fly. And again, bees. Zapping your brain, the TV
on to help you sleep. This is only a game,
theory. Sleep in the off-season. Dream.

DESTROYER

It was chasing him through the forest
near his house, dogging him through the salal
and undergrowth, through the swamp
across the ditch towards the beach.
It was gaining on him, he could feel it
breathing not far behind, its shadow
nipping his heels. All he could do
was keep on running, tripping on roots,
keep on moving, busting through cobwebs.
Flies stuck to his forehead and arms
and stinging nettle stung his legs,
and devil's club clawed his feet,
and ticks dropped starving on his scalp
but still he could not stop, its heat
then burning his back, his skin
blistering and breaking open. He was
screaming but he could not hear himself
as he burst onto the beach, it was with him
then searing the sand to glass,
stealing his traction, his grip, he began to falter,
first his feet sliding out from under him,
then his thighs collapsing like water,
his palms hydroplaning in front of him,
and he knew he was going to die falling—

And a fiery hand reached down
and torched his hair soft as smoke
and branded his flesh with lips and ears and a nose,
and welded his skeleton with iron
to make it strong, and melted his skin
until it was smooth as an eyeball,
and breathed fire into his throat
to fill him with passion,
and kindled a flame in his skull
so he'd always have light and he'd never stop
burning with thoughts and he'd never stop
burning, feverish in the fist of love.

The City Through the Treetops

Short climb to the crown where the branches curtain back
and like that it rises through a trap door in the horizon:

a colossal contraption of wheels and pulleys and simple
machinations, carefully staged and cantilevered by mountains:

the harbour freighters scrape into place and the clouds in the
            rafters
shift and articulate. It's the whole apparatus in gear before us:

the cars on their tracks commanded by magnets; the birds on
            the booms
who trapeze between buildings. And there, through a tear

in the fabric, the eye of the child who spies us and smiles.

Hexagonal by conception. Archeological
pit-work in reverse: rebar and steel girders
rigged and raised by jig and counterweight,
patched together with prefabricated cards
of concrete craned into place, then wired
and plumbed for water and heat. Cells are
assigned by relative mobility: those most
likely to survive a sixteen-storey dive versus
those most likely to survive the staircase.
We call it the beehive or the honeycomb,
the way our lives are patterned, droned,
confined to six-sided cavities we either rent
or lease but rarely own. Rules state no
pets please over the weight of a cigarette.
Ours is a culture of cyber-optic connection
and closed-circuit cameras enciphered
in the ceiling. Strata Council would like to
note that the sprinklers are not meant
as shuriken. In the event of an emergency
the axe in the glass case may be used
at the tenant's discretion. Listen: tightrope
walkers, base-jumpers, trapeze artists,
tricksters with slight-of-height-or-gravity
numbers, get your shows on the road and
in front of our windows. Back-lit, this glass
façade barely exists, save the aluminum
mullions that divide my place from his.

THE LETTER

Years after you fixed the postage with a kiss
printed my name and residence in tiny blue sticks
and sent it off through the lips of the mail slot,

it arrives again at the bottom of a dusty shoebox,
faded and creased like the voice of the deceased
on someone's ill-forgotten answering machine,

bundled unceremoniously with telephone bills
and bank receipts, the postmark putting you in Dublin
on St. Patrick's Day, a week shy of our third

anniversary. Where was I that night? At home
holding forth at the toilet bowl after a dose too many
in your memory, no doubt, or wrapped up

in the curtains having a go at the ghosts we'd chosen
over pets or children . . . It's not a question
I can answer for certain, anymore than what happened

the moment the envelope left your possession:
whether the man in the black sedan caught a flash
of your skirt as you stepped from the curb or

the shriek of his brakes the last thing you heard.

Last Night on Earth

A twilight moth is a passing thought and crickets are exquisite
music boxes, tiny, spring-loaded and taut

Over your house the stars are tied-off dogs frenzied at their stakes
every minute howling rockets across the blackening ache

And quiet between the walls spiders sow their eggs
web-stitch their babies and prim their legs

Now your cheekbone chisels your flesh, erupts in your skin
Now your wrist reveals its delicate detail, its witching trick

Another electricity eels your body, burns out the filament of your
        heart
recharges, recharges, restarts it

To see you like Michelangelo would emerging from the rock
To see the life-stone that unhatched you sloughed off.

RIVER VIEW

You leave the house and walk
towards the water. The city you live in
is built on floodplain and farmer's field,
flat as the ancient world, when all was balanced
on the shell of a turtle. The land you walk is
below sea level, yet the road slopes
towards water. All log boom and tugboat,
small fingers of wood, you fix the river's shape
in your mind, its glassy mathematics,
how it happens so quickly,
paced between hummingbird and midnight.

The clammy spill of moon on your neck,
like a blade laid flat against skin.
You're all goose-pimple and runny nose
as you stroll the quay. You stop
and stars swim like mackerel into your pupil.
Kneel and tie your sneaker.
For a moment you wonder why you are here
and not at home, in bed with your lover.
You begin to remember,
I left the house and walked towards the water. . .
You begin to remember,
then you forget,

steal a dinghy from a ship
called *It's Real*, and row into the river,
eyes shut, pulling away
from the shore. Apartment lights
leak through your eyelids.
You heard the word
and it sounded like *river.*
I left the house and the boat's taking on water. . .
You hear it now.
Row harder, it says. *Row harder.*

THE ISLAND HIGHWAY IN WINTER

Rain-netting. Wipers working overtime,
lolling you to sleep in the passenger seat
like a pair of black mechanical sheep,
and me gripping the wheel and high beams
trailing twin tunnels of light along a cut
in the mountainside, the what-has-been
and where-from sucked up and sealed
as we leave it behind in the deepening night.
A fight just to stay awake, to focus
my eyes on the road, not get distracted
by the shadows of elk and wolves
we imagine moving at the treeline,
the slink of the cougar's spine threading
the edge of the headlights, an owl diving
a ditch for rodent and coming up fowl.
A slash of asphalt we've travelled all
our lives when heading home, when leaving
what we know now in favour of what we knew
then. The car shaking in the buffeting wind
as I press the pedal a little harder, unable
in the dark to name or label exactly where
we are but anxious to get there a little faster
just the same. Hard to believe in the daylight

a fist of broken knuckles ranges above
us and hawks hunt in scrub brush
at the roadside. I've often thought
of dying while passing on this highway,
shifting into a slick of ice on the bridge
over Englishman River and steering into
the plunge—but that's neither here nor there,
or at least not yet, your slumped head resting
in a nest of hair against the window, deep
breath spreading like petals across the glass,
like hoarfrost over the passing black.

ACKNOWLEDGEMENTS

First, Melanie Willson.

Second, my family, especially my mother, Tina Rader, and my grandparents, Albert and Margaret Rader, who taught me to love words.

Then Matthew Hooton, Doug Harrison, Chris Hutchinson, Don McKay, Russell Thornton, Elizabeth Bachinsky and Silas White for their influence on these poems. A special thanks to Ben Didier for the cover design.

Then everyone from those miraculous hours: a book of matches for you all.

Earlier versions of many of these poems first appeared in the following publications: *sub-TERRAIN, Grain, Pine, Prism International, Disclaimer, The Prairie Journal, Geist, Event, The Malahat Review, Breathing Fire 2: Canada's New Poets* (Nightwood) and *The Land Beyond* (greenboathouse books). Thanks to the editors of each.

The epigraph is from Mark Strand's "In Celebration" from his book *The Story of Our Lives* (Knopf). Copyright © 1973, 2002 by Mark Strand.

The italics in "Diviner" are from Patrick Friesen's poem "The Man Who Invented Himself" from his book *Unearthly Horses* (Turnstone). Copyright © 1984 by Patrick Friesen.

The title "The Island Highway in Winter" is a paraphrase of Terence Young's "The Island in Winter" from the book of the same name (Signal). Copyright © 1999 by Terence Young.

This book remembers Rodney Mitchell, Jan Dayman and Sarah Lambillon.